SILENCE RIVER

Antônio Moura
SILENCE RIVER
R I O   S I L E N C I O

ॐ

Translated by
Stefan Tobler

Introduced by
David Treece

Arc
PUBLICATIONS
2012

Published by Arc Publications,
Nanholme Mill, Shaw Wood Road
Todmorden OL14 6DA, UK

Design & cover photograph by Tony Ward
Printed in Great Britain by T.J. International Ltd,
Padstow, Cornwall

978 1906570 67 5 (pbk)
978 1906570 68 2 (hbk)

ACKNOWLEDGEMENTS
The poems in this book have been selected from
Hong Kong & outros poemas (Hong Kong & Other Poems),
Ateliê Editorial, 1999;
Rio Silêncio (Silence River), Lumme, 2004; and
A sombra da Ausência (The Shadow of Absence), Lumme, 2009.

This book was published with the support of the
Ministry of Culture, Brazil / National Library Foundation.
Obra publicada com o apoio do Ministério da Cultura do Braxil /
Fundação Biblioteca Nacional.

MINISTÉRIO DA CULTURA
Fundação BIBLIOTECA NACIONAL

Supported using public funding by
ARTS COUNCIL
LOTTERY FUNDED | ENGLAND

Arc Publications 'Visible Poets' series
Editor: Jean Boase-Beier

CONTENTS

SERIES EDITOR'S NOTE

The 'Visible Poets' series was established in 2000, and set out to challenge the view that translated poetry could or should be read without regard to the process of translation it had undergone. Since then, things have moved on. Today there is more translated poetry available and more debate on its nature, its status, and its relation to its original. We know that translated poetry is neither English poetry that has mysteriously arisen from a hidden foreign source, nor is it foreign poetry that has silently rewritten itself in English. We are more aware that translation lies at the heart of all our cultural exchange; without it, we must remain artistically and intellectually insular.

One of the aims of the series was, and still is, to enrich our poetry with the very best work that has appeared elsewhere in the world. And the poetry-reading public is now more aware than it was at the start of this century that translation cannot simply be done by anyone with two languages. The translation of poetry is a creative act, and translated poetry stands or falls on the strength of the poet-translator's art. For this reason 'Visible Poets' publishes only the work of the best translators, and gives each of them space, in a Preface, to talk about the trials and pleasures of their work.

From the start, 'Visible Poets' books have been bilingual. Many readers will not speak the languages of the original poetry but they, too, are invited to compare the look and shape of the English poems with the originals. Those who can are encouraged to read both. Translation and original are presented side-by-side because translations do not displace the originals; they shed new light on them and are in turn themselves illuminated by the presence of their source poems. By drawing the readers' attention to the act of translation itself, it is the aim of these books to make the work of both the original poets and their translators more visible.

Jean Boase-Beier

From where he lives, in a high-rise apartment block in downtown Belém, a city of one and a half million inhabitants, Antônio Moura can see the surrounding Amazon rainforest, a wide muddy bay formed by a tributary of the Amazon river, and the lush green crowns of the old mango trees that provide much-needed shade in the main square, the Praça da República. He can see all this, and readers from abroad or from Brazil's centres of cultural power, Rio de Janeiro and São Paulo, might hope to read about this in his poetry – not about urban life in the Amazon (no one wants to read about that) but rather poems rich in the region's flora and fauna, its indigenous customs. After all, as the inhabitants of Belém and Manaus joke, people from the rest of Brazil expect to see crocodiles slinking round the streets (there are only stray cats and dogs) and one might expect this to be Moura's 'Unique Selling Point' for people who don't know the Amazon. It was also what I originally hoped for: with the rich world of the Amazon on his doorstep, wouldn't it be a waste not to let it inhabit the poet's imaginative world? What I didn't realize was that the specifics of Amazonian nature and folklore had already been used so widely in local, regional literature that some contemporary writers had simply had enough of what was becoming a poetic straitjacket.

Moura and most urban Amazonians are Westerners in two ways: the lawlessness and cheapness of life in Belém or Manaus might be today's Wild West, but the local culture also courses with many of the same cultural energies as Europe and North America, and Moura is not going to deny this. It cannot be by chance that Moura has chosen to live in a 26-storey modernist building which stands at the heart of this large city. The landmark Manoel Pinto da Silva building owes its functional use of reinforced concrete and economy of form to Le Corbusier's architecture, and possibly owes its sinuously curving balconies to Oscar Niemeyer's visual language. It is a building of which the city is rightly proud and yet the pride is tinged with nostalgia. It was said to be one of the two dozen tallest buildings in the world when it was constructed, a symbol of the city's sense of progress.

That sense is little felt these days and the once new building, while still beautiful, is old enough to have become haunted by its own ghosts; it is infamous as a place from which people have launched themselves to their deaths. If a certain disillusioned affection for modernism is a response to this building, could it describe Moura's poetic position too?

Much poetry in the Anglophone Western world is full of the details of places and things. This has become particularly pronounced since the Imagists and others reacted against the rhetorical extravagances of late Victorian verse. Ezra Pound's 'Go in fear of abstractions' is widely known and respected, as is William Carlos Williams' 'no ideas but in things', which has now been plucked out of a poem to serve as a dictum for creative writing workshops. The influence of Pound and North American verse is now increasingly strong in Brazil too. Yet Moura's poetry is written in a more pared-back vocabulary than such poetry of detail; he prefers the generic terms to the specific, for example in the poem 'In line with the anonymous will' (p. 47) where he lists: "tree / body, insect, rock, water, star / wind, cloud, moon, sun...".

Moura's poems, if they appear strange to a reader of this selection, are not strange because they are Brazilian, or Amazonian, but because they are unexpected, because they sometimes disrupt speech's syntax, and because he has increasingly taken his own route forward. His later work is far from any school's prescriptions.

Of course, he shows affinities with certain poets, such as Baudelaire, Dylan Thomas (after whom one of his cats is named), Georg Trakl (mentioned in 'The Refugee' (p. 81)), and the Franco-Egyptian poet Edmund Jabès. His poetry also sometimes echoes that of the two poets he has translated: the Peruvian César Vallejo (his 'Considering coldly, impartially' (p. 45) uses lines from a poem by Vallejo, as the endnotes mention) and the Madagascan Jean-Joseph Rabearivelo. Certain schools of poetry have evidently taught him much, such as the Concrete poetry of the late 1950s and 1960s as made by poets such as Haroldo de Campos and his brother Augusto de Campos, as well as the

10

Brazilian Constructivist poetry that followed it (Régis Bonvicino is an important name associated with Constructivist poetry). Constructivist poems are not the arrangements of a few words or syllables on the page that the clean Concrete poems were, but they take up Concrete poetry's emphasis on the poem's visuality and concision and its interest in deconstructing words phonetically to find other words. As with the Concretists, the connection to modern visual art is also important. In this Preface I will confine myself largely to my reading and how that has shaped my translation. I have translated Moura's poetry as a body of related poems, not as individual, self-contained units, and so would suggest that any attempt to read horizontally across the facing pages will not be a fulfilling reading experience. My choice of a word or phrase has often depended on how it chimes with other images and themes in his poetry.

Moura's second collection, *Hong Kong & outros poemas* (*Hong Kong and Other Poems*), published in 1999, made a great impact on the Brazilian poetry scene. Its words are precise, a sharpened knife that cuts through cliché, worn-out language and the acceptable surface of our society to reveal violence and commerce, yet it is also incredibly playful in its syncopated rhythms and syntax. It shifts to the side our expectations, makes phrases strange, or cuts them up, collages different perspectives. There is a violence done to language in the poem 'In a Station of the Metro' (p. 27) which is the desire to renew language: "a shot (astray) defoliates / the bullet the rose of the crowd". Of course, in riffing on Pound's poem, Moura explicitly alludes to his modernist forebears, and he again alludes to them in the poem 'Déjeuner sur l'herbe' (p. 33) which is not only the name of a Manet painting, but of Picasso's re-workings of that painting.

Hong Kong is in the line of Brazilian Constructivist poetry mentioned above. We see this in Moura's visual use of white space on the page and in the dollar signs in the sky in 'Hong Kong' (p. 25) – are they in the shape of a cross? The Southern Cross? Geometric shapes also often appear in Constructivist poetry, suggesting an approach to the abstract art of the original

Russian Constructivists and in 'Déjeuner sur l'herbe' in the present collection there are both circles and a triangle'. Continuing the constructivist vein, we also see a deconstruction and reconstruction of words in the *Hong Kong* poems. In the poem 'Hong Kong' itself, the adjective *"vendados"* (blindfolded) is taken apart in the next line's *"à venda"* (for sale), while a little later *"prega"* (which as a verb means 'proclaims', or 'preaches', or 'nails', and as a noun means 'a pleat' or 'a fold') re-appears in the word *"pregão"* (meaning a proclamation, or bidding, or the trading of stocks). In order to work in a similar way in English, rather than using 'for sale', I chose the also commonly read "Sold", which echoes "blindfolded" in its sound. Similarly, of the various possibilities for *"prega"* I went for "proclaims" which as well as working semantically, by suggesting the "hubbub-market" and its noise, allows the word to modulate into "claims" (which has appropriate financial connotations). In 'Photo Album' (p. 29) there is a play of sounds that comes to the fore in the translation of *"dialogam loucos"* ([they] dialogue, [are] mad) as "discuss and cuss". "Cuss" is not directly present in the Portuguese, but has been chosen for its sense of discord, as well as its suitability in recreating the poet's tight use of sound patterning and repeated syllables in his early poems.

Moura's third and fourth collections, *Rio Silêncio* (*Silence River*) and *A sombra da ausência* (*The Shadow of Absence*) continue to mould the material of language to its visual appearance on the page. They also reject the position that experimental or avant-garde poetic techniques are incompatible with older poetic forms, such as couplets. There must have been some head-scratching when *Rio Silêncio* appeared. Where *Hong Kong* was a kaleidoscope of shifting angles and colours, the collections that followed have the clarity and urgency of black and white woodcuts (a different form, but not necessarily any less modernist).

In these two later collections death becomes a central concern. The poems are more probing in their thoughts, angrier at times, more grief-stricken. There is less space left for lighter play; instead there is a powerful mythic reach, as seen in the child in

'Once Long Ago' (p. 61) who "hid herself under roots and stones in the earth" and the bizarre Neo-Baroque worlds of poems such as 'When the blue rain hurls' (p. 53) and 'After the Flood' (p. 57). Rather than a societal vision of commerce and violence, as in the earlier 'Hong Kong' and 'In a Station of the Metro', life appears now as something uncanny and mysterious that the individual must face. The sense of a tension between opposing poles becomes more prevalent: between spiritual insight and the dirty realities of life; between the contemporary and previous eras; between the wider picture and the intensely personal. Or are they such opposites? The individual is merely an instrument of "nature's indecipherable purposes" in 'Father' (p. 67), while the first line of another poem, 'Reduced to his size by the blue size of the sky' (p. 55), inverts our commonplace ideas of scale: the sky fits snugly when it "falls coat over his shoulders". In 'Walking home, usual routine' (p. 69), the poet's first name becomes an adjective describing the poem's addressee; the poem is addressed to a you, who is antônio.

As the phrase "falls coat over his shoulders" and the neologistic use of his name as an adjective both show, Moura continues in these later collections to be open to language that is not colloquial and to techniques and styles that owe much to the experimentation of (for want of a better term) the avant-garde. The willingness to make language strange continues in the third and fourth collection, although there is no sense that Moura feels a poetic obligation to do so at all times. 'Stains' (p. 63) shows an understated use of visual poetry. The final colon iconically represents a person and a bird. The Portuguese draws this out by saying "*Ave e homem, dois pontos*" (bird and man, two points / dots). "*Ponto*" can mean 'point' or 'dot' (eg the dot on an 'i'), and "*dois pontos*", as well as meaning 'two points' or 'two dots', is the Portuguese term for 'colon'. "Two dots" (rather than 'two points') leaves the poem open to the typographical meaning in English. English offered many other felicities, such as finding that the final word of 'The Shadow of Absence' (p. 83), which in Portuguese is "*habita*" (inhabits), could in English be both inhabit and be alive: the "light lives".

I hope this little insight into the translator's reading will help above all to enrich an understanding of Moura's poetry, as the translation process has certainly enriched mine. For any readers wishing for some help in understanding the Portuguese of Moura's poems, there are some endnotes, which also reveal the pernickety attention to detail that is the translator's joy and curse. Moura's poetry is above all a pleasure to read, and I hope the endnotes will unlock some of the subtleties of the Portuguese.

It has been exciting for me to translate Moura's poetry, which questions contemporary assumptions about poetry and about our lives. I am curious to see where his poetry will lead next, and how contemporary poets might respond to it. While language is often inadequate, a "hubbub", a "deaf sound", words can also be our home and refuge, as Moura's 'The Refugee' puts it:

> Without an aim, he passes through strange tongues, carrying
> lit in his mouth all his treasure: a language.

Stefan Tobler

INTRODUCTION

The poetry selected and translated here brings to the eyes and ears of English-speaking readers an intensely distinctive and compelling voice; indeed, for all the paradoxical implications of the title, Antônio Moura's *Silence River* is striking evidence of the enduring power of poetry in early twenty-first century Brazil as voice, as the invention and performance of a discursive persona, an idiom whose diction, attitude and philosophy of life may move or challenge but which, above all, 'speaks to us'. If this apparently conventional approach to the craft is surprising in a poet from one of the 'emerging powers' of the new millennium, better known these days for its postcolonial urbanity and cool chic, then that is certainly worthy of note.

For a civilization such as Brazil's, one so resonant with the rhythms and intonations of popular speech, tradition, and music itself, over the last hundred years its poetry has been remarkably, we might say disproportionately, in thrall to programmatic, academic or avant-garde agendas, and as a consequence its roots in the communicative power of the speaking voice have sometimes seemed remote and forgotten. The Modernists of the 1920s fought the first battles on behalf of the vernacular language 'of the street', as both a renewed blow for national independence from the cultural legacy of Portuguese colonialism, and an anti-elite gesture of solidarity with the popular classes and their traditions. But the natural, colloquial ordinariness of Carlos Drummond de Andrade and Manuel Bandeira had to compete, too, with the more self-consciously experimental agenda of Oswald de Andrade's Brazil-Wood Poetry and its 'telegraphic' concision, recalling contemporary media such as journalism and photography; with the frenetic Futurism and stream-of-consciousness exuberance of Luis Aranha and Mário de Andrade; with the folkloric and neo-indigenist epic narratives of the nationalists, or with the mysticism of the Catholic revivalists.

A new wave of avant-garde movementism was unleashed in the 1950s with the Concretists' radical abstract objectivity, breaking entirely with the notion of poetry as expression and discourse, in favour of 'verbi-voco-visual' form-as-content.

Against the backdrop of technocratic developmentalism and its left-wing critiques, the theory and practice of poetry became ever more dichotomised between rival projects and polarised positions: formalist abstraction vs. social commitment and didacticism, cosmopolitan universalism vs. regional tradition, post-industrial poetry for the consumerist urban masses vs. protest in verse for the popular classes.

But not everyone was absorbed by, or reduced to, these competing and seemingly antagonistic orthodoxies, with their often dogmatic and prescriptive theory and rhetoric. Even if closely associated with one or other tendency in their formative years, the strongest and most consistently original voices of the second half of the century managed to steer independent paths for themselves. Whether João Cabral de Melo Neto, the master of objective rigour in the most traditional of verse forms, relentlessly interrogating the elemental vocabulary of human experience, the peasant-poet's labour with earth and words; or the erstwhile Neo-Concretist and 'Street-Guitar' protest poet Ferreira Gullar, reclaiming a lyrical language stained by experience in 'Poema Sujo' (Dirty Poem); or Armando Freitas Filho, bringing together the intellectual, linguistic and formal discipline of the early 1960s avant-garde movement known as 'Praxis', and the underground 'Marginal' poets' dramatic, real-time engagement with the biography of experience under dictatorship during the 1970s: all these poets transcended the sterile polarisations of their time, which set the aesthetic and the social, or print and speech, in opposition to one another, and instead they discovered a creative and critical tension in the dialogue between the discipline of formal structure and the social dynamic and meaning of language as communication. Above all, they staked their commitment to explore, transform and reinvent the material resources of their craft, to renew the Portuguese language.

To his great credit, Antônio Moura stands squarely within that same heterodox tradition of self-possessed engagement with, yet independence from, the powerful currents and counter-currents that have swept and ordered the literary field in Brazil across much of its recent history. But there is a further imperative that Moura's poetry laudably resists, which has to do with another, geographical, dimension of Brazil's cultural politics: the tension between the country's economic and political centre of gravity (the Southeast axis linking São Paulo, Rio de Janeiro and Minas Gerais) and other competing regional or local identities in the South, Centre-West, Northeast or North – the latter including Moura's own Amazonian state of Pará. It is not hard to imagine the pressure or expectation facing writers in Moura's position to shoulder the regionalist burden and stake out an equatorial, jungle alternative to the various literary and folkloric dialects disputing claims to national authenticity from other corners of the territory.

While a longstanding tradition of Amazonian 'regionalism' certainly does exist, there are nonetheless also powerful precedents, in prose fiction at least, for any writer intent on avoiding the obvious temptations to folklorise or stereotype local identity. So while Márcio Souza has satirised the madness of 'savage capitalism's' unexpectedly precocious assaults on the region in the early twentieth century, Milton Hatoum has patiently narrated the sagas of immigrant life that, drawing on his own family's biographies, have connected the social history of the city of Manaus with that of Lebanon.

Yet when it comes to Antônio Moura's poetry, thematic references to his native state of Pará and its capital, the port city of Belém, or even to the vocabulary and imagery of Amazonia's cultural landscape, appear to be entirely absent. Certainly, in his ongoing quasi-philosophical reflections on the unfolding drama of human experience, Moura is not especially concerned with the topicality of the Amazonian scenario, its sociological, environmental or mythical associations.

Nevertheless, there is one key topos of *Silence River* for which it would be hard to find a better setting or objective correlative on earth, and that is the confrontation between nature and humanity. Except that, in Moura's world, that nature, far from being the uncharted, virgin Garden of Eden of post-colonial Amazonian mythology, is instead our age-old habitat, the inescapable locus of our alienated human condition. As his 'Song of Exile' (p. 77) suggests, to live is like "feeling a brief exile", exiting and re-entering one's house "without knowing if we are / inside or outside, / (the moon and the sun as neighbours)". In the concentrated, brief compositions before us, which display his talent for throwing an intensely focused light on the immediate, powerfully suggestive image or idea, Moura invites us to stop, pause and dwell on the suspended scenes, episodes, moments – still-lives – in man's endless wanderings through that existential habitat that we call the world,

> remembering that the day
> is a fistful of powder from stars
> that the night scoops and hurls
> onto eyelashes before sleep,
> that the sky has a violet sound over
> this man's hair as he works in the setting sun
> with the smell of gunpowder on his hands
> and that this same man, when he enters
> his lover, wants, perhaps, to return

('Considering coldly, impartially', p. 45)

Often, the revelatory instant is masterfully captured, like the minute detail in a Bruegel painting, in such a way as to lay bare our collective dismay and perplexity at the materiality we are irresistibly and clumsily caught up in. As in 'Fall' (p. 51):

> When the sound of a fall is
> heard and on running to the spot
>
> stretched out and alone, exposed,
> a soul is found, victim of its own body,
>
> his open eyes staring into space,
> the sky is for him, almost dead,
>
> a blue bruise on the shoulders of
> the world that, human animal, approaches

18

sniffing and forming all around
a wall, a ring of whispers,

ohs and ahs exchanging surprised looks
and caught up in this game, they forget

the being that, fallen, is still breathing, and if
this being, inert, hints at movement

or a sigh escapes his lips, the world
around, instead of offering a hand,

runs, cowardly, every which way,
colliding with each other

The fallen individual gazing up at the sky is just one variation
on a recurring figure, which finds the human being suspended
between earth and heaven, between the realm of material,
unconscious existence and its perceptual contemplation; another
version is the symmetry between man and bird, two minuscule
marks caught in each other's field of vision as they move across
ground and sky:

The stain that floats and
the stain that crawls along,
but which also rises when
the sight of the bird lends it wings.
Stain bound in the grass, observing
the black stain suspended in the blue,
both come from the world's secret womb
to the insecurity of nature's seen face.

('Stains', p. 63)

It is important to understand that the natural realm is not here
a metaphor for the human; rather, human experience is the
universe in microcosm, projected, writ large across the canvas
of its macrocosmic counterpart:

Oh, yes, miniature existence,
this little walk every day

19

as you return, antônio and nocturnal
to your home, miniature of another home

– whole, universe, that waits behind night

('Walking home, usual routine', p. 69)

And it is out of that analogous convergence between natural
history and human history – between the concentric circles of
sky, setting sun, ripples, and the erotic turning of "the turf / at
the gates of your / triangle garden" ('Déjeuner sur l'herbe');
between the "House-womb which we left / to enter the womb-
house of / four walls where we arrive" ('The House'); between
our body's temporal endurance and the experiential duration
of life's journey ("A day to cross – sun / between two immense
nights, / having as company the body, / that humble beast that
doesn't / belong to you and which, without / a question, offers
itself, devotedly / to time, god who is also / the very body in its
silence", 'Crossing', p. 39) – it is out of that relational threshold
of correspondence and analogy that is crystallised the poetry
of meaning, the creative act of signifying and communicating.
Nowhere is that liminal, creative moment, the birth of speech,
more beautifully suggested (nor more sensitively rendered into
English by translator Stefan Tobler) than in 'The Wait' (p. 41):

Waiting, standing, on the rock,
between the sea's green sphere

and the star that nears
every night, you speak

more and more mutely,
with a voice that listens to the bottom

of another voice that comes
and saysandoesn't in an echo,

in uh? seaweed language,
a wee bit like this deaf sound:

nada, dressed in body and karma
while the world dissolves

After all, if, in Antônio Moura's vision, nature and humanity can be revealed as coextensive realms, analogous dimensions of a single, commensurate order, then it is because our human faculties alone are capable of giving meaning and voice to the world. As we are reminded so succinctly and eloquently in 'Signs' (p. 79), it is the particular "form" of our senses that determines how the rustling of the wind in the leaves or the waves crashing on the rocks are heard and made "sonorous in the conch of the ear" –

All the world's din is an inner rippling.
Outside, life moves in the deepest silence.

David Treece

from
HONG KONG & OTHER POEMS
HONG KONG & OUTROS POEMAS

HONG-KONG

a Edson e Fátima Secches

Paira
    sobre as cabeças
uma alta quantia de estrelas

Na terra
      olhos vendados
onde se lê grafitado: *à venda*

Sob
o céu
esticado
     – tenda –
o burburinho-mercado
prega
(pregão)
a milhõe$
     $
          $
       $
     $
       $
de planetas

(nuvens com etiquetas)

à noite
    o sol é ouro especulado

HONG KONG
for Edson and Fátima Secches

Hovering
          over our heads
a high number of stars

On earth
          blindfolded eyes
where you read in graffiti a *Sold*

Under
the stretched
skies
     – a tent –
the hubbub-market
proclaims
(its claims)
to million$
          $
                    $
               $
          $
                    $
of planets

(clouds with pricetags)

to the night
          the sun is speculators' gold

NUMA ESTAÇÃO DO METRÔ, *around*
1916 d.c., a aparição das
faces na multidão, pétalas
num ramo escuro úmido,
dilata a pupila de Ezra,
enquanto outra turba
(a mesma?) se despetala:
um tiro (a esmo) desfolha
a bala a rosa da multidão,
numa estação do metrô,
1998 d.c.

IN A STATION OF THE METRO, *around*
1916 AD, the apparition of
these faces in the crowd, petals
on a black humid bough,
dilates Ezra's pupil,
while another throng
(same one?) de-petals:
a shot (astray) defoliates
the bullet the rose of the crowd,
in a station of the metro,
1998 AD

ÁLBUM

Vai-se, esvai-se o clã

o pai
    a mãe
        o irmão
            a irmã
Vão-se
os gatos
Vão-se
os cães

Volta?

Enquanto

o dia e a noite
dialogam loucos
quedando os torsos
        à tua porta

PHOTO ALBUM

A clan parts, departs

father
        mother
                sister
                        brother
The cats
depart
The dogs
depart

Returns?

Meanwhile

day and night
discuss and cuss
leaving their torsos
                    at your door

O JARDIM DO PALÁCIO
a Marta

No princípio
tuas iris
      – águas

onde boiaram
minhas iris
      – algas

sob arcos
árabes: tuas
duas pálpebras

Agora

varando arcos,
águas, ardo

  – silêncio –

entre as palavras

THE PALACE GARDEN
for Marta

Right at the start
your irises
            (of water)

in which my irises
            (of seaweed)
were floating

under Arab
arches: your
twin eyelids

Now

passing arches,
waters, I'm burning

– silence –

between words

ALMOÇO NA RELVA

Do céu fechado
(semi-
círculo)
sobre o
lago
cai verde
uma gota de ave
         – excremento –
abre n'água
cír   círculos
concêntricos

O lago, outro
círculo

verde
circundado
por mais verde avermelhado
pelo círculo do sol
poente

relva onde talo teso gramo

às portas do seu
triângulo jardim

DÉJEUNER SUR L'HERBE

From the cloud cover
(semi-
circle)
over
the lake
one drop of what
falls green
            – a bird´s dropping –
opens in water
in concentric
cir   circles

the lake, another
circle

green
surrounded
by more green reddened
by the circle of the sun
setting

lawn where I stalk dig hard

at the gates of your
triangle garden

from
SILENCE RIVER
RIO SILENCIO

A MÃO QUE ABRE O LIVRO MUNDO
escreve folhas e folhas de árvores.
Lê, com olhos na ponta dos dedos,
o alfabeto de estrelas que se apaga
a cada página virada.

A CASA

Ventre-casa de onde saímos
para entrar na casa-ventre de
quatro paredes onde chegamos.
Um entre, onde ficamos em
convívio: pai, filho, espírito, espanto
quando um a um de nós caímos
no tumulto do mundo, largados
à miragem de estar sozinho,
até ver a imagem no espelho
que reflete o invisível, até ouvir
o indizível chamado para
voltar ao ventre, casa
sem uma única parede entre as estrelas
de onde, talvez, nunca tenhamos saído

THE HAND THAT OPENS THE WORLD ITS BOOK
writes full pages and pages of leaf.
Read, with eyes on fingertips
the alphabet of stars that goes out
with every turned page.

THE HOUSE

House-womb which we left
to enter the womb-house of
four walls where we arrive.
A halfway, where we live
together: father, son, spirit, wholly
surprised when one by one we fall
in the world's turmoil, abandoned
to the mirage of being alone
until we see the image in the mirror
that reflects the unseeable, until we hear
the unspeakable call for us
to return to the womb, house
without a single wall between the stars
which, perhaps, we have never left

TRAVESSIA

Um dia para atravessar – sol
entre duas noites imensas,

tendo como companhia o corpo,
este pequeno animal que não

te pertence e que, sem nada
perguntar, se oferece, devotadamente,

ao tempo, deus que também é
o próprio corpo em silêncio

Um dia para transpor tendo por alimento
a poeira da estrada que se estende

branca, do nascente ao poente e
que, lentamente, transforma-se em

riacho negro que passa sob a
ponte suspensa da Via Láctea

Ir, à outra margem, de acordo
com o que a própria ida engendra

Ora com o silvo das serpentes sob o passo
Ora andando sobre as águas do poema

CROSSING

A day to cross – sun
between two immense nights,

having as company the body,
that humble beast that doesn't

belong to you and which, without
a question, offers itself, devotedly

to time, god who is also
the very body in its silence

A day to get across, having for food
the dust on the road that stretches

white, from where the sun rises to where it sets,
and that, slowly, transforms itself into a

black stream that flows under the
suspended bridge of the Milky Way

To go, to the other bank, according
to what the going itself engenders

At times with the hissing of serpents underfoot
At times walking on the water of the poem

A ESPERA

À espera, de pé, na pedra,
entre a esfera verde do mar

e a estrela que a cada
noite se aproxima, falas

cada vez mais mudo,
numa voz que escuta o fundo

de outra voz que vem
e diz-não-diz em eco,

hein, idioma de algas,
algo assim num som surdo:

nada, vestido de corpo e carma,
enquanto se dissolve o mundo

THE WAIT

Waiting, standing, on the rock,
between the sea's green sphere

and the star that nears
every night, you speak

more and more mutely,
with a voice that listens to the bottom

of another voice that comes
and saysandoesn't in an echo,

in uh? seaweed language,
a wee bit like this deaf sound:

nada, dressed in body and karma
while the world dissolves

CONVITE À SOMBRA

Debruçado sobre a página
a mercê de sua sombra que,

por trás, à traição, traz o punhal,
enquanto escreve segundo a voz

e a vontade da palavra que lhe
vem para ser oferta de repasto

e convite à sombra para sentar-se
à mesa e repartir o mesmo pão que

o diabo amassou sob olhar divino
– trigo do inferno, fornos do céu –

em aliança na noite floresta
infestada de insetos e estrelas

INVITATION TO THE SHADOW

Bent double over the page
at the mercy of your shadow

that behind you, betraying you, holds
a dagger as you write by the voice

and the will of the word that comes
to you to be offered as a feast

and invitation to the shadow to sit
at the table and share the same hard bread

kneaded by the devil under God's watchful eye
– hell's wheat, and heaven's ovens –

allies in the night, forest
infested with insects and stars

CONSIDERANDO A FRIO, IMPARCIALMENTE,
que o homem é triste, tosse e, no entanto
se acomoda em seu peito avermelhado,
que ele nada mais é do que compor-se
de dias, que é lúgubre mamífero e se penteia,
considerando isso e lembrando que o dia
é um punhado de pó de estrelas
que a noite, com sua pá, atira
sobre as pálpebras de sono,
que o céu tem som violeta sobre os
cabelos deste homem que trafega no poente
com cheiro de pólvora nas mãos
e que este mesmo homem, quando penetra
em sua amada, quer, talvez, voltar
Que o sol é a solidão às claras
Que a lua é um búzio numa toalha gralhazul
gargalhando o destino em crateras
Que a sombra que nasceu comigo
espera de meu corpo um gesto que
ela possa, com amor, repeti-lo
Que o silêncio dos noivos é a voz do Amor
procurando uma boca por abrigo
e que as palavras dos que não se entendem
não são mais palavras mas sanguessugas na língua
Que, entre dentes, a Roda da Fortuna mastiga o Fracasso
e que o diabo bebe as suas fezes sorrindo ao meu lado
Lembrando que amanhã, pela manhã talvez,
o mar venha desfazendo meus membros de areia e
me fazendo lembrar que, ao mesmo tempo,
não lembro de nada, a não ser de um ventre

CONSIDERING COLDLY, IMPARTIALLY
that man is sad, coughs and yet
settles for his reddened chest,
that he is nothing more than composed
of days, is a lugubrious mammal and combs himself,
considering this and remembering that day
is a fistful of powder from stars
that the night scoops and hurls
onto eyelashes before sleep,
that the sky has a violet sound over
this man's hair as he works in the setting sun
with the smell of gunpowder on his hands
and that this same man, when he enters
his lover, wants, perhaps, to return
That the sun is loneliness without the shadow of a doubt
That the moon is a conch in a magpie-blue cloth
laughing into its craters over its fate
That the shadow that was born with me
waits for a movement from my body so that
she can, lovingly, repeat it
That the silence of a couple is love's voice
looking for a mouth to shelter in
and that those who don't understand each other
don't have words but leeches on their tongues
That, between its teeth, the Wheel of Fortune chews each failure
and that the devil sits smiling beside me drinking his shit
Remembering that tomorrow, tomorrow morning,
the sea could start to crumble my limbs of sand and
remind me that, at the same time,
I don't remember anything, except perhaps a womb

CONFORME A ANÔNIMA VONTADE
que se mostra como isto – um

vazio de silêncio e ruídos
onde nos encontramos partes

de um que dividido em árvore
corpo, inseto, pedra, água, estrela

vento, nuvem, lua, sol que se põe
sobre tudo isso que se parece com estar

vivo, acordando e dormindo um
quando em que os olhos abertos ou

fechados não tornam tudo muito
distinto, conforme esta vontade

enlaçamos nossas mãos e seguimos,
aparências, desaparecendo no caminho

I N LINE WITH THE ANONYMOUS WILL
that shows itself like this – a

void of silence and noises
where we find we are parts

of one that divided into tree
body, insect, rock, water, star

wind, cloud, moon, sun that sets
on all of this that looks like being

alive, waking and sleeping a
while in which eyes, opened or

closed, don't make everything very
clear, in line with this will

we join hands and carry on walking,
appearances, disappearing on the path

ONICANÇÃO

Tão grande que
para se ver tem
que fazer de seus
próprios olhos dois
espelhos: céu e mar

Tão sem par que
para ter com quem
falar tem que ouvir
a própria voz em
tudo se manifestar

A ONDE VAI A VOZ QUE DAQUI SAI
ao encontro de algo ou alguém

que a si talvez também não se
saiba quem ou o que entre árvores

gatos, cães, moedas, moenda
solar triturando a noite e suas

estrelas – pó estelar que se
acumula sobre as pálpebras

através dos dias até que um dia,
(ao fechar as pálpebras) cai e se des

faz, sem voz, na luz cotidiana

OMNISONG

So wide that
to see itself
it has to turn
its own eyes into
mirrors: sky and sea

So without equal that
to have someone
to talk to, it has to
hear its own voice
spoken by all things

W HERE DOES THE VOICE GO THAT LEAVES
to find something or someone

that perhaps also doesn't know
who or what among trees

cats, dogs, dollars, the solar
mill grinding the night and its

stars – ground star that
gathers on eyelids

over days until one day,
(when the eyelids close) it falls and dis

integrates, voiceless, in the everyday light

QUEDA

Quando ouve-se o som de uma
queda e correndo-se ao encontro

acha-se estirada e só, ao relento,
uma alma vítima de seu próprio corpo

e, olhos abertos fixos para o espaço,
o céu é para este quase morto um

azul de hematoma sobre os ombros do
mundo, que, bicho humano, aproxima-se

farejando e formando ao redor
um muro círculo de murmúrios,

ohs e ahs entreolhando-se com espanto,
e, entretidos neste jogo, esquecem-se

do ser que, caído, ainda respira ali, e se
este ser, inerte, esboça um movimento

ou de sua boca sai um sopro, o mundo
ao redor, em vez de um gesto de socorro,

corre, covarde, para todos os lados,
dando-se de encontro uns aos outros

FALL

When the sound of a fall is
heard and on running to the spot

stretched out and alone, exposed,
a soul is found, victim of its own body,

his open eyes staring into space,
the sky is for him, almost dead,

the blue of a bruise on the shoulders of
the world that, human animal, approaches

sniffing and forming all around
a wall, a ring of whispers,

ohs and ahs exchanging surprised looks
and caught up in this game, they forget

the being that, fallen, is still breathing, and if
this being, inert, hints at movement

or a sigh escapes his lips, the world
around, instead of offering a hand,

runs, cowardly, this way and that,
one colliding with another

QUANDO A CHUVA AZUL ARREMESSA
pedaços de céu contra as vidraças,
abro as janelas de água e entre
vejo-te nas gotas, centaura de ouro,
fisgo teu eco boiando em cavernas vazias

Na torre de doçura que o fruto edifica,
nos navios em chamas à flor da espuma,
nas luvas de nuvem que a noite usa
em suas unhas negras, sinto teu Sim
e teu Não respirando, teu beijo arfando

no fundo do jardim submarino, que eu,
disfarçado em cão marinho, farejo com fôlego felino,
animando as algas para um rito de sal ao som
das violas que as ondas solam em cordas de areia

Criança feiticeira, um rubi posto em tua testa
te ilumina as mãos sangradas por estrelas e espinhos
ao tocarem a haste noturna que sustém a rosa da aurora

Aroma do universo fecundado nos abismos

WHEN THE BLUE RAIN HURLS
bits of sky against the panes,
I open the windows of water and
glimpse you in drops, a gold she-centaur,
I catch your echo floating in empty caverns

In the sweet tower that the fruit raises,
in the ships blazing on the cusp of the foam,
in the cloud gloves that the night uses
over its black nails, I feel your Yes
and your No breathing, your kiss gasping

at the bottom of the underwater garden that I,
dressed as a marine dog, sniff out, exciting
the seaweed into a salty rite to the strumming
of chords that the waves are playing on strings of sand

Witch child, a ruby set on your forehead
illuminates your hands, bloodied on stars and thorns
from touching the night stem that lifts dawn's rose

Scent of it all, of the universe seeded in abysms

R EDUZIDO AO SEU TAMANHO PELO TAMANHO AZUL DO CÉU
que cai manto sobre os seus ombros
ele caminha

entre flores, excrementos, alfabetos e o enxame de estrelas
zumbindo ao redor
de sua cabeça

Suas asas de anjo – para cima

abrindo-se à vertigem da altura e
e à possibilidade do baque
da queda

Sua carcaça de bicho – para baixo

farejando o sangue transmitido por
noites de núpcias e uma constelação
de acasos

(o centauro pai beligerando-o sobre a relva mãe ao duro golpe de
[seus cascos)
trazendo

à flor da terra, em sua vontade cega, ele, um talo,
que às vezes pensa
ter algum poder

como o de – ora veja – apagar e acender o dia
num piscar de olhos

R EDUCED TO HIS SIZE BY THE BLUE SIZE OF THE SKY
that falls coat over his shoulders
he walks

between flowers, faeces, alphabets and the shoal of stars
buzzing around
his head

His angel wings – opening

up to the vertigo of the height and
to the possibility of the impact
of a fall

His beast's carcass – sniffing

down the blood transmitted
by wedding nights and gathered
random events

(the father centaur making him and war on him, on the mother
lawn with hard blows from his hooves)
carrying

to the surface of the earth, in his blind will, a stalk,
that he sometimes thinks
has some power

such as that of – get this – turning the day off and on
with a blinking eye.

APÓS O DILÚVIO

Pela manhã, após o dilúvio, a lama nas calçadas,
os cacos de trovões no chão, o silêncio branco

do céu ensopado em gaze, as casas de lodo
e as alamedas disparando seus alarmes, os

caranguejos caindo dos ninhos das árvores
e as aves, no solo, querendo refazer o vôo

ao peso do barro e das h'eras sobre as asas,
o navio encalhado no topo de um telhado,

os animais estátuas sob a argila crosta à beira
do mar morto de sede bebendo vento nas mãos

em concha da areia, os jardins, Ó, os jardins
desabrochando em lodo, o sangue das crianças

jorrando das torneiras dos palácios e correndo
em sargetas para os esgotos, o sol lambendo

a pele das cobras que — relâmpago — agora
mudam de casca e pendem entrelaçadas

nos parapeitos dos edifícios entre as flores entre
abrindo as pálpebras de musgo para o arco-íris

refletido nos olhos do rosto sobrevivente,
que aspira o ar, ainda úmido, após o dilúvio

AFTER THE FLOOD

The morning after the flood, mud on the pavements,
splinters of thunder on the ground, white silence

of a sky soaked in gauze, the mired houses
and the avenues setting off their alarms, crabs

falling from nests in the trees and
birds on the ground trying to recreate flight

with the weight of the muck and ivies
on their wings, a ship stranded on a rooftop,

animals turned to statues under the clay crust
by the sea dying of thirst drinking wind from hands

that form cups of sand, the gardens, oh the gardens'
slime blossoms, the blood of children

spraying from taps in the palaces and running
along gutters to the drains, the sun licking

the bodies of the snakes that – flash of lightning – now
change their skin and hang entangled

from the balconies of buildings between flowers half-
opening their mossy eyelids to the rainbow

reflected in the eyes of the surviving face
that breathes in the air, still humid, after the flood

QUANDO

Quando a luz cegar o seu fio
de navalha que corta tudo em

claro e escuro, e esta sombra
já não tiver a centelha com que

dialogar alternando-se em sol
e lua, silêncio e palavra, terra

e céu refletido nas águas do rio que
arrasta a imagem das noites e dos dias,

quando por mero acaso repentino
ou ocaso lento e gradual romper-se

o fio de voz que traz o não e o sim
na mesma frase de ritmo imprevisível,

nada ao mundo faltará e nada se
abalará a este pequeno movimento

de asa, que, ao decolar, vibra,
imperceptivelmente, a folhagem

WHEN

When light dulls its filament thin
knife edge that cuts everything into

bright and dark, and this shadow
no longer has a spark for mutual

exchange, alternately sun
and moon, silence and word, earth

and sky reflected in the waters of the river that
drags the image of the nights and days,

when a mere sudden chance
or slowly dimming change breaks the filament

thread of the voice that carries no and yes
in the one phrase's unforeseeable rhythm,

the world will lack nothing and nothing
will rock at this little movement

of a wing, that on taking off, shakes,
imperceptibly, the foliage

ERA UMA VEZ

A Criança e a Sombra brincavam
de ser Um ao sol – por todo o dia
corriam juntas até caírem abraçadas
no sono sobre a relva à margem da noite

Um dia veio a Voz Trovão, que despertou
num susto as Irmãs que dormiam amalgamadas:
A Sombra camuflou seu corpo na pele da escuridão
A Criança escondeu-se sob as raízes e as pedras no chão

Da separação brotou um homem.
Que as vezes ouve no fundo de si uma voz:
a Criança e a Sombra chamando seu nome

ONCE LONG AGO

The child and shadow would play
at being one in the sun – all day long
running around until in each other's arms
they fell asleep on the lawn at the edge of the night

One day a thundering voice came, and scared
awake the two sisters who slept, blurred together:
the shadow camouflaged her body on darkness's skin
the child hid herself under roots and stones in the earth

From their separation a man blossomed.
Who sometimes hears, deep inside himself, a voice:
the child and the shadow calling his name

MANCHAS

Uma pequena mancha preta ave no topo do dia.
O dia que se ergue do sono das estrelas.
Ave sobre a terra e suave se aninha
nas retinas do homem que, pequenino,
entrecerra os olhos lançados para cima.
Uma pequena mancha na terra
e uma pequena mancha no céu,
espelhando-se em suas imagens provisórias.
A mancha que flutua e
a mancha que se arrasta,
mas que também se eleva quando
a visão da ave lhe empresta asas.
Mancha presa na relva mirando
a mancha preta suspensa no azul,
vindas do ventre secreto do mundo
para a incerteza da face visível da natureza.
Mancha celeste, mancha terrena.
Entre elas apenas o rumor do vento
segreda a poeira e a nuvem da existência.
Pequenas manchas pretas sobre o branco do dia.
Ave e homem, dois pontos, à beira do silêncio:

STAINS

A little black stain bird at the top of the day
The day that rises from the stars' sleep.
Bird above the earth and whirring to nest
on the retinas of the man who, so small,
half-closes his eyes as he looks up.
A little stain on the earth
and a little stain in the sky,
reflecting each other in provisional images.
The stain that floats and
the stain that crawls along,
but which also rises when
the sight of the bird lends it wings.
Stain bound in the grass, observing
the black stain suspended in the blue,
both come from the world's secret womb
to the insecurity of nature's seen face.
Heavenly stain, earthly stain.
Between them just a murmur of wind
whispers dust and the cloud of existence.
Little black stains on the white of the day.
Bird and man, two dots, on the edge of silence:

RESIDÊNCIA

Ao pisar o jardim da casa
cuidado para não afundar

os pés até os tornozelos fincando
fundas raízes no chão, apegado ali,

estátua plantada entre flores,
não haverá como ir ao mar

quando assolado pelo verão,
nem voltar ao calor do leito

se flagelado pelo inverno
Vivemos partindo de uma morada

que se ergue em todo lugar com
telhas de nuvem e paredes de vento

Não há o que abandonar quando,
caracol inverso, levamos a casa dentro

HOME

Stepping into the house's garden
take care not to sink

in up to the ankles, driving
roots deep into the ground, attached,

a statue planted between flowers,
there will be no way to go to the sea

when laid to waste by the summer,
nor to return to the heat of the bed

when lashed by the winter
We live leaving a dwelling

that rises up in every place with
tiles of clouds and walls of winds

There is nothing to abandon when,
inverse snails, we carry our homes within

PAI

Tudo isso se baseia em que a espécie,
onde está a raiz do nosso ser, possui sobre nós
um direito mais imediato e anterioque o indivíduo.

– ARTHUR SCHOPENHAUER

Tua mão de espuma já desfeita na areia
Tua orelha em concha no fundo do mar
O tambor de tua têmpora e de teu quadril
batendo no dia em que centauro
galopou, galopou, galopou,
sobre a rosa tatuada em fogo no ventre de minha mãe,
despetalando-a
Quando eu do fundo da sombra te chamava
e tu, ingênuo, sem saber que me buscavas
com uivos e olhos possuídos pelo gênio oculto
que a tudo atropela pelo seu intento:
o de trazer, através de um sopro, um vento,
um ser para vagar cego entre cegos
num labirinto de ecos e sinais secretos
onde também é – por um sopro,
um vento – desfeito a qualquer momento
Pai, nada a fazer senão estender
a mútua mão do perdão diante
dos propósitos indecifráveis da natureza:
Tu, por, inconsciente, me fazeres,
desamparado, entrar no tempo
Eu, por te fazer, sem escolha, meu instrumento

FATHER

This is because the species,
in which lies the germ of our being,
has a nearer and prior claim upon us than the individual.
— Arthur Schopenhauer

Your hand is foam undone in the sand
Your ear a conch at the bottom of the sea
Drums of your temples and your hips
beating on the day when you centaur
galloped, galloped, galloped
over the fire-tattooed rose of my mother's womb,
de-petalling her
When I called you from the depths of a shadow
and you naively, unknowingly, looked for me
with howls and eyes possessed by the hidden spirit
that knocks over everything in its intent
to bring, through a gust, a wind,
a being to drift blindly among the blind
in a maze of echoes and secret signs
where at any moment – by a gust,
a wind – it can be undone
Dad, nothing for it but for both
to hold out a hand in forgiveness, faced
with nature's indecipherable purposes:
You, for, unwittingly, making me
enter time, without support or hold,
I for making you, without choice, my instrument

A CAMINHO DE CASA, ROTINEIRAMENTE,
após o suor do pão amassado pelas

mãos de Deus e do diabo, os astros
por cima, os restos dos mortos por

baixo dos pés que caminham com
muito cuidado para não perturbá-los,

o vento roçando a fronte e o tempo
pisando as têmporas, patas de cavalo

arrastando à galope as rosas do amor
para um outro caminho, não este

por onde vens diariamente sozinho, entre
rostos alheios – entre eles o de alguém que

não veio – sentindo o cheiro da sombra dos
que passaram e pressentindo as sombras

que uma esquina antes desapareceram e
com teus olhos jamais se encontraram.

Ah, pequena réplica da existência,
solidão, este curto caminho cotidiano

por onde voltas antônio e noturno para
casa, pequena réplica de outra casa

– o Universo, que atrás da noite aguarda

Walking home, usual routine,
on your brow the daily sweat

for bread baked by God and the devil,
stars above, remains of the dead

below your feet that walk
carefully to not disturb them,

the wind brushes your forehead and time
treads your temples, horse's hooves

drag love's flowers off at a gallop
to another road, not this one

that you come up every day, among
strange faces – one is of someone

who didn't come –, you sense the smell
of the shadows of people who passed

and disappeared a corner earlier,
who your eyes won't ever meet.

Oh, yes, miniature existence,
this little walk every day

as you return, antônio and nocturnal
to your home, miniature of another home

– whole, universe, that waits behind night

F EITO ISHMAEL EM MOBY DICK,
sempre que sinto na boca uma

amargura crescente, sempre
que há em minha alma um

novembro úmido e chuvoso
é tempo de fazer-me ao mar.

E munido de quase nada, só
da palavra que é puro sopro,

através dela inflo a vela e parto
em dois o ar e a água que levam

a asa da alma e o casco do corpo
ao encontro do belo monstro

que acena do horizonte com seu
olhar verde e vivo: o Desconhecido,

o sempre bem vindo irmão-
gêmeo da criação, ladrão do fogo

lançando envolto em nuvens
pelas frestas dos aposentos

o seguinte clarão: toda a água
em volta da casa já está estagnada,

pasto para hordas de mosquitos.
E, ouvindo isto, feito Ishmael

parto em dois o mar – poema
sempre a um passo do abismo

Turned Ishmael in Moby Dick,
whenever I find myself growing grim

about the mouth, whenever
it is a damp, drizzly

November in my soul,
it is time to take to sea.

And armed with next to nothing, just
the word that is almost less than a breath

a gust with which I fill the sail and part
in two the air and the water that carry

the soul's wing and the body's hull
to meet the beautiful beast

that beckons from the horizon with
his gaze green and lively: the Not-known,

the always most welcome, twin-
brother of creation, the stealer of fire

surrounded by clouds who throws
through the windows of my lodgings

the following flash: all water
around your house is stagnant

pasture for hordes of mosquitoes.
And hearing, turned Ishmael

I part the sea in two – the poem
always one step from the abyss.

NUM LIVRO DE SAN JUAN DE LA CRUZ

Entre as páginas de um livro de
San Juan de La Cruz deparo

com a vida entrelaçada à morte ao
acaso, entre a vida que ali floresce

em palavras, voz humana que
no deserto em branco se propaga,

o corpo morto de um inseto entre
as páginas fala do que pode estar

sendo e – num relâmpago – ter sido,
fogo abafado pela mão desconhecida

que, subitamente, fecha o livro

IN A BOOK BY SAN JUAN DE LA CRUZ

Between the pages of a book
by San Juan de la Cruz I find

life and death entangled quite
by chance, in the midst of life that flourishes

there in words, a human voice that
propagates in the desert's white,

the dead body of an insect between
the pages speaks of what can be

being and – in a flash – have been,
a fire put out by an unknown hand

that, all of a sudden, closes the book

from
THE SHADOW OF ABSENCE
A SOMBRA DA AUSENCIA

SEM TÍTULO

O pássaro está mudo.

Isto que aqui canta é
apenas sua sombra.

Só

a sombra do pássaro
canta as penas do pássaro

mudo – e só – sobre o muro

CANÇÃO DO EXÍLIO
a Paulo Ponte Souza

Viver – sair,
dar a volta ao

redor da casa e
entrar pela saida,

sem saber se estamos
dentro ou fora

(a lua e o sol por vizinhos)

E como – às vezes – parece
que demora - Viver

é experimentar um breve exílio

Almada, inverno 2004

UNTITLED

The bird is silent.

What is singing here is
simply its shadow.

Only

the bird's shadow
sings the sorrows of the bird,

silent – lonely – on the wall

SONG OF EXILE
for Paulo Ponte Souza

Living – leaving,
to go once

around the house and
enter by the exit,

without knowing if we are
inside or outside,

(the moon and the sun as neighbours)

And how it– sometimes – seems
to drag – living

is feeling a brief exile.

Almada, winter 2004

INDÍCIOS

A natureza reina silenciosa.
O rumor do vento nas folhas
e a onda que bate na rocha
enchendo sonora a concha do ouvido,
outros sons teriam – vento, onda –
se outra fosse a forma dos sentidos.
Todo o barulho do mundo é um marulho interior.
Fora, a vida move-se sem o menor rumor.

ESBOÇO

Teu rosto se insinua nos contornos desta linha.
Por detrás da renda negra das palavras
a estrela de teus olhos palpita.
Um fio de teus cabelos serpenteia rio
por entre as pedras, sílabas.
E a imagem do que nunca vi, visita-me.

SIGNS

Nature reigns in silence.
The rustle of wind in the leaves
and the wave that smacks on the rock
sonorous in the conch of the ear,
would have other sounds – wind, wave –
if the senses' forms were other.
All the world's din is an inner rippling.
Outside, life moves in the deepest silence.

SKETCH

Your face slips into the contours of this line.
Behind the words' black lace
the pulsing star of your eyes.
A strand of your hair snakes river
between the stones, the syllables.
And the image of what I've never seen, visits me.

O REFUGIADO

A Stefan Tobler

À janela – uma cortina de fumaça e fogo.
À porta – uma estrada de fumaça e fuga.
No jardim, a flor da morte mina subterrânea.
A noite violada procura seus filhos nos escombros.
Uma criança caminha, de encontro à besta que se aproxima.
Sem pai nem mãe o dia abala para longe.
Sem rumo, passa por estranhas línguas, levando
aceso dentro da boca todo o seu tesouro: um idioma.
Entre o seu olhar e o olhar dos seus – bombardeada – desaba a ponte.
Um novo estrondo – as estrelas caem
e os cacos de céu ferem-lhe os ombros.
Um sol abatido à tiros tomba no Leste.
Um trovão intolerante ira seus relâmpagos.
O fantasma de Trakl volta a lastimar o mundo Grodek.
Ao som de um órgão enevoado,
da boca em chamas do crepúsculo, um coro
sobe e queima o céu da Europa:
"Sou um refugiado, moro numa casa
de cinzas ao vento, por favor, um abrigo".
Ecoa, entre as nuvens, um enorme silêncio boquiaberto

Paris, verão, 2004

80

THE REFUGEE
for Stefan Tobler

At the window – a curtain of smoke and fire.
At the door – a road of smoke and flight.
In the garden, the flower of death, underground mine.
The violated night hunting for her children in the debris.
A child walks, towards the beast that nears.
Without father or mother the day bolts, into the distance.
Without an aim, he passes through strange tongues, carrying
lit in his mouth all his treasure: a language.
Between his gaze and the gaze of family – bombed – the bridge collapses.
Another explosion – the stars fall
and the shards of sky wound his shoulders.
A sun downed by gunfire in the East.
An intolerant thunder brings lightning to a rage.
Trakl's ghost returns to mourn the Grodek world.
To the sound of a snowy organ,
from dusk's mouth in flames, a chorus
rises and burns Europe's sky:
"I'm a refugee, I live in a house
of ashes in the wind, a shelter, please."
Echoing, between the clouds, an enormous open-mouthed silence

Paris, summer 2004

A SOMBRA DA AUSÊNCIA

O corpo vai, a sombra fica.
Um eco sem voz que assombra

a sala, a mala sendo arrumada
para a viagem, que, dia-a-dia

se faz um pouco sem saber se
é volta ou ida – O copo quebra,

o sabor fica, a aura de um hálito
em torno à boca que se intensifica,

quando um conhecido fantasma
passa pelos terraços da memória

e evoca um nome, um aroma, uma
hora perdida entre as folhas secas

de um outono que se deteriora
conforme a mão do inverno o toca.

O céu se ensombra, o azul fica.
Em alguma dobra das pálpebras

da íris, dos cílios, sua luz habita

THE SHADOW OF ABSENCE

The body goes, the shadow remains.
An echo without voice that haunts

the room, the case already being packed
for a journey, that, day by day

is taken a little without knowing if
it is a return or one way – The cup breaks,

the taste remains, the aura of a breath
around the mouth, that intensifies

when a familiar ghost
passes along memories' terraces

and evokes a name, an aroma, an
hour lost between the dry leaves

of an autumn that falls apart
as winter's hand touches it.

The sky darkens, the blue remains.
In some fold of the eyelids,

of the iris, lashes, its light lives

TRANSLATOR'S ENDNOTES

'Silence River': The third collection's title, *Rio Silêncio*, and my translation of it, *Silence River*, is also the title given to this selection in English. The Portuguese title is composed of two nouns: *rio* is 'river', *silêncio* is 'silence' not 'silent', which would be *silencioso*. The position of *silêncio* after *rio* suggests it could be the name of the river (just as the River Thames is *Rio Tamisa* in Portuguese), but there is also a second possible meaning, that *silêncio* functions here as an adjective (particularly as *silêncio* ends with an -o, the commonest ending of an adjective that agrees with a masculine noun, such as *rio*). In English the first option (of *silêncio* as a river name) would be translated as River Silence, the second (of *silêncio* as an adjective) would be translated as Silence River. I have opted for the second option, because it is the option that preserves the strangeness of the Portuguese. In English, when the noun 'river' is placed before another noun it qualifies it (eg riverboat, riverbank), and the phrase sounds very everyday, so River Silence would have sounded like a twee description of silence at a river, a caption for a misty photo. This would have been unsuitable for Moura's poetry.

pp. 26-27 'Numa estação do metrô': "*a aparição das / faces na multidão, pétalas / num ramo escuro úmido*": this is a quotation from one of the Portuguese translations of Ezra Pound's poem 'In a Station of the Metro'.

pp. 32-33 'Almoço na relva': this is also the title most commonly used in Portuguese to refer to the Manet painting most commonly referred to in English discussion as 'Déjeuner sur l'herbe'. Picasso created cartoonishly erotic versions of this painting, and Moura's poem continues the process with its own eroticism.

The word "*ave*" is chosen rather than the more common word for bird: "*pássaro*". Choosing "*ave*", the line in Portuguese sounds almost the same as the phrase "*uma gota de água*": a drop of water.

pp. 36-37 'A casa': "*espanto*" (surprise) is very close to "*santo*" (saint, holy), and so this line almost says "*espírito santo*" (Holy Spirit).

pp. 40-41 'A espera': "*falas*" is in the second person '*tu*' verb form, which is the informal 'you' in the Portuguese from Portugal, and is used in some parts of Brazil, including Pará, Moura's home state.

The word *"hein?"* means "huh?" / "what?", but the 'h' is silent, so *"hein"* / êj / sounds very much like / ẽ / *'em'* (meaning: in).

pp. 42-43 'Convite à sombra': *"comer o pão que o diabo amassou"* (to eat the bread the devil kneaded) is an idiomatic expression that means 'to have it tough' / 'to lead a dog's life'. Here in a Manichean twist the forces of good and evil are more balanced, allies even, as the devil kneads the bread under a divine gaze. See a similar twist to the expression in *'A caminho de casa, rotineiramente'* ('Walking home, usual routine').

pp. 44-45 'Considerando a frio, imparcialmente': this poem is a homage to César Vallejo, whom Moura has translated, and sets off from some lines from Vallejo's poem *'Considerando en frío, imparcialmente'*.

The *'gralha-azul'* (cyanocorax chrysops), called the azure jay in English, is an iridescently blue and black bird, inhabiting forests from the southern part of the state of Rio de Janeiro down to Rio Grande do Sul, the most southerly Brazilian state. *'Gralha'* is a term for some birds of the Corvid family; *'azul'* is the common Portuguese word for blue. Here *"gralhazul"* is contracted into one word, and placed after the noun, used as an adjective.

pp. 46-47 'Conforme a anônima vontade': The verb *'parecer'* is 'to seem', 'to appear'. *'Se parecer estar'* would be 'to seem to be', while *'se parecer com'* means 'to look like' / 'to be similar to', and is followed by a noun, to compare things or people. Moura confabulates the two constructions into the phrase *"se parece com estar"* (to look like to be), which is not everyday Portuguese. *"Quando"* means 'when', and is not normally used as a noun as it is here (a when). However, as *"quando"* ends with -o, the common ending for masculine nouns, it is less surprising than 'a when' would be.

pp. 48-49 'Aonde vai a voz que daqui sai': there is the expectation of finding a verb after the *"quem ou a que"* or before the dash, for example *'não se saiba quem ou o que é'* (doesn't know who or what

85

it / he / she is). Instead the question up to the dash is a fragment, an incomplete question.

pp. 52-53 'Quando a chuva azul arremessa': *'centauro'* would be centaur, by substituting the -o with a feminine ending -a, Moura's *"centaura"* is a female centaur.

"Cão marinho" could be translated literally as 'sea dog', however there is no suggestion in the Portuguese phrase of a sailor.

pp. 54-55 'Reduzido ao seu tamanho pelo tamanho azul do céu': *"beligerando-o"* combines the invented verb *'beligerar'* and *'o'*, which is 'him'. The neologism *'beligerar'* is made up of *'gerar'* (to produce, conceive, engender) and *'beli-'*, relating to war.

pp. 60-61 'Era uma vez': child (*criança*) and shadow (*sombra*) are both feminine nouns in Portuguese, which leads into the idea that they are sisters (*irmãs*).

pp. 62-63 'Manchas': *"ave"* (bird) is normally only a noun. It can be read as an unpunctuated clarification of the stain, if *"ave"* is the start of a second half of the sentence that does without a comma or article. Yet in this poem it can also be read as if it were a verb: this would create a syntactic sentence and is suggested by *"ave"* ending in -e, one of the three regular endings for a third person singular verb in the present tense (-a, -e, -i). The same suspicion of *"ave"* as a verb is found in line 3.

pp. 68-69 'A caminho de casa, rotineiramente': see note above to 'Convite à sombra' ('Invitation to the Shadow') referring to a similar twist to the idiomatic phrase *'comer o pão que o diabo amassou'* (to eat the bread the devil kneaded).

"Antônio" is not a Portuguese adjective, only a name. However, its small *'a'* in the text, its ending in *'o'* (the normal ending of a masculine adjective), and the fact that it is linked to an adjective (nocturnal), all suggest it is used here as an adjective.

pp. 70-71 'Feito Ishmael em Moby Dick': from *"sempre"* to *"mar"* is an abridged quote from Berenice Xavier's translation of the first page of *Moby Dick*: *"Sempre que sinto na boca uma amargura crescente, sempre que há em minha alma um novembro úmido e chuvoso, [...] é tempo de fazer-me ao mar"*. The English original

86

reads: "Whenever I find myself growing grim about the mouth; whenever it is a damp, drizzly November in my soul […] I account it high time to get to sea as soon as I can."

pp. 72-73 'Num livro de San Juan de La Cruz': like Spanish, Portuguese has two different verbs where in English we simply have 'to be'. *Estar* is used to express temporary locations and variable mental or physical conditions, for example to say 'I'm home', 'I'm happy'. *Ser* is used for permanent locations and characteristics (or which relatively speaking appear more permanent: I'm a translator, he's a Catholic, they are a great couple).

Moura plays here with these two ways of being. "*Sendo*" and "*ter sido*" (on the following line) are forms of ser ('being' and 'to have been' respectively). "*O que pode estar // sendo*" is translated as "what can be // being". In Portuguese the stanza break between the first and second verb for 'to be' of this gerundial phrase serves to emphasize the different possibilities. In this poem the apparently more permanent state of being (*ser*) is shown as precarious, and subject to change in our daily present. The fly is busy being, but then is no more. (Its fire is put out as the book is closed, the moment of reading is a temporary life; a closed book is dead, until re-read).

pp. 76-77 'Sem título': "*pena*" in Portuguese can mean feather or quill, as well as suffering, sorrow, travail. The line could also be 'sings the feathers of the bird'.

BIOGRAPHICAL NOTES

ANTÔNIO MOURA was born in 1963 in Belém, capital of the state of Pará, in the Brazilian Amazon, where he now lives, working in an advertising agency, after periods in São Paulo and Lisbon. While Brazil has a strong tradition of regionalist writing, his work cannot be seen in this way. He does not feel a duty to use the Amazon as his subject matter, as a good regionalist would. His poetry started in the Brazilian avant-garde tradition that is often called Constructivist poetry, and which developed from Concrete poetry. Yet his shelves are also lined with European poets: Dylan Thomas provided the epigraph to his latest collection, Georg Trakl is another companion, and French-language authors are particularly important to him, from Pascal and Baudelaire to Edmund Jabès. Four collections of his poetry, and three of his translations, have been published: his collections *Dez* (1996), *Hong Kong & outros poemas* (1999), *Rio Silêncio* (2004) and *A sombra da ausência* (2009), and his translations of the Madagascan poet Jean-Joseph Rabearivelo, *Quase-sonhos* (2004) and *Traduzido Da Noite / Traduit De La Nuit* (2009), and of the Peruvian César Vallejo, *Contra o segredo profissional* (2005).

His poems have appeared in many Brazilian journals and newspapers, as well as in a number of contemporary anthologies in Brazil and abroad. He is currently being translated into Spanish, Catalan, German and English. Earlier versions of some translations in this collection have appeared in the UK journals *Shearsman* and *Modern Poetry in Translation*, as well as in *Crossing / Travessia*, a pamphlet from the São Paulo small press Arqueria Editorial.

STEFAN TOBLER is a freelance translator from Portuguese and German, and has recently established the new not-for-private-profit publisher And Other Stories, which focuses on contemporary international fiction. Its first books include Villalobos's *Down the Rabbit Hole*, shortlisted for the 2012 *Guardian* First Book Award, and Levy's *Swimming Home*, shortlisted for the 2012 Man Booker Prize. His translation of Roger Willemsen's *Afghan Journey* (2007) was a Recommended

Translation from English PEN and his first translations of Antônio Moura were awarded the BCLA John Dryden Translation Prize's commendation in 2008. His most recent translation from Portuguese is of *Água Viva*, the most poetic book by the great Clarice Lispector. His own poems and prose have appeared in journals such as *Shearsman*, *Ambit*, *The Wolf* and *nth position*.

DAVID TREECE received his BA in Hispanic Studies (1982) and his PhD in Brazilian literature (1987) from the University of Liverpool. Between 1984 and 1987 he worked for the human rights NGO Survival International and produced a report on the impact of a major Amazonian development project, the Greater Carajás Programme, on the region's indigenous communities. He continued his interests in the politics and social impact aspects of Amazonian development by contributing to film documentaries and to the activities of the NGO Brazil Network.

In 1987 he joined the Department of Portuguese and Brazilian Studies at King's College London. Since 1989 Treece has been an Associate Fellow of the Institute for the Study of the Americas (formerly Institute of Latin American Studies), University of London, teaching on its MA programmes every year. From 2000 he was Associate Fellow of the University of London's Institute of Romance Studies and a teacher on its MA programme and, since 2001, an Advisory Council member of the *Programa Avançado de Cultura Contemporânea*, Federal University of Rio de Janeiro. In 2000 Treece was awarded the Order of Rio Branco by the Brazilian Government for services to Brazil-UK relations.

Treece was co-founding editor of the *Journal of Latin American Cultural Studies* (*Travessia*) from 1992 to 2004, he has been a co-editor of Portuguese Studies since 2005, and is a Committee member of the Modern Humanities Research Association, and a member of the editorial boards of the *Bulletin of Latin American Research*, *Legenda* and the *Journal of Romance Studies*.

Also available in the Arc Publications
'VISIBLE POETS' SERIES
Series Editor: Jean Boase-Beier

No. 1 – MIKLÓS RADNÓTI (Hungary)
Camp Notebook
Translated by Francis Jones, introduced by George Szirtes

No. 2 – BARTOLO CATTAFI (Italy)
Anthracite
Translated by Brian Cole, introduced by Peter Dale
(Poetry Book Society Recommended Translation)

No. 3 – MICHAEL STRUNGE (Denmark)
A Virgin from a Chilly Decade
Translated by Bente Elsworth, introduced by John Fletcher

No. 4 – TADEUSZ RÓZEWICZ (Poland)
recycling
Translated by Barbara Bogoczek (Plebanek) & Tony Howard,
introduced by Adam Czerniawski

No. 5 – CLAUDE DE BURINE (France)
Words Have Frozen Over
Translated by Martin Sorrell, introduced by Susan Wicks

No. 6 – CEVAT ÇAPAN (Turkey)
Where Are You, Susie Petschek?
Translated by Cevat Çapan & Michael Hulse,
introduced by A. S. Byatt

No. 7 – JEAN CASSOU (France)
33 Sonnets of the Resistance
With an original introduction by Louis Aragon
Translated by Timothy Adès, introduced by Alistair Elliot

No. 8 – ARJEN DUINKER (Holland)
The Sublime Song of a Maybe
Translated by Willem Groenewegen, introduced by Jeffrey Wainwright

No. 9 – MILA HAUGOVÁ (Slovakia)
Scent of the Unseen
Translated by James & Viera Sutherland-Smith,
introduced by Fiona Sampson

.